On Sale

How Retailers Ignore
Their Numbers
and Give Their Store Away

Cathy Donovan Wagner

On Sale: How Retailers Ignore Their Numbers and Give Their Store Away

ISBN 978-1-940170-64-0

Printed in USA by 48HrBooks (www.48HrBooks.com)

Dedication

This is for all of you who have a dream and want to make a difference. This is for my God who put this dream in my heart and holds my hand in this journey. Thank you to Patty Donovan Hunt, Sandy Rienks, Marc Weiss and Suzanne Evans for showing me how to birth that dream and teach my experiences to help others. Thanks to Keely Shaw and Kelly Epperson for lending their skills to this. It does take a village. Thanks to my Most Fun Family kids: Caitlin, Colleen, Clare and Christopher! This wouldn't have happened without you. And to my beloved Paul – thanks for loving me.

Table of Contents

About the Author

With over 26 years of experience in retail as both an owner and a consultant, Cathy Donovan Wagner has the unique position of having worked on both sides of the counter. She has seen firsthand the tremendous benefits that the strategic planning and inventory management processes bring to a business. It is what helped her to grow to 3 stores grossing in excess of 2.5 million dollars.

She sold her stores to be able to help other retailers implement these processes, uncover hidden opportunities and create business growth. Cathy's private clients continuously see more profit and develop more cash flow than the previous year. Cathy's passion as The RETAIL Maven is to help retailers develop action plans that increase sales, improve cash flow and create success...and love their life!

Cathy's guidance has helped countless retailers achieve the financial and career freedom to spend more time with their families. She recalls, "My oldest entered a nationwide contest run by Money Magazine and Cranium. She talked about some of the funny traditions we do, like we all go to see Santa and get pies in our faces on our birthday. We won and were named America's Most Fun Family.

We were interviewed all over, and were provided our own PR people for a while. We went on TV and radio talking about our crazy traditions."

The systems Cathy developed and shares with indie retailers every day through RETAILMavens gave an entrepreneur with a multi-location, multi-million dollar business the freedom to put the fun in being a family, develop traditions, and develop a sense of family identity – all without sacrificing her retail dream!

Preface

"To love what you do and feel like it matters, what could be more fun." Katherine Graham, former owner, publisher, and CEO of the *Washington Post*

I completely disagree.

To love what you do and feel like it matters and **make money,** what could be more fun?!

While this concept is nothing new, it has overwhelmed retailers since the beginning of time.

Retailers aren't profitable and they aren't loving their lives. It's stupid. It happens because they don't pay attention to their numbers. They stick their head in the sand and complain about the weather rather than take responsibility to learn what they need to and develop a strategy to fix it. That is what this book is about.

Let's be clear. It's not about sales training, It isn't about advertising. It's not about merchandising or managing a sales team.

This book is for retailers who are sick and tired of not getting the success they want AND want to learn how to change. It's for retailers who are afraid of numbers and retailers who love numbers. Most often, neither of you know which numbers to look at. It's for retailers who have cash flow but *never seem to have money*.

I want you to learn how to manage the cash that goes through your hands and make sure that there is more for you to keep. That is what cash flow and profit is all about.

Put this down if you have all the money you want and wouldn't know what to do with more.

For sure, close this book if you have an ego so big that you don't see how pointing your finger and blaming someone or something else makes three fingers point back at you. Those three fingers are a gift from God telling you that there were three things you could have done to change the situation.

If you are a whiny and complaining type, you won't want to read this either. (But you probably should.)

I am going to share with you what you have to do. Fill out the worksheets. Write in this book. Own it. Change will happen for you as you work this process.

I have been there, done that, failed, and succeeded. In these pages, I share with you the science of retail. It is a whole different approach to how to be truly successful in your retail life, without having to learn the hard way like I did.

Introduction
The Journey of the Accidental Entrepreneur

"What people call serendipity sometimes is just having your eyes open." Jose Manuel Barroso

I never thought I would be a retailer.

Following in my dad's footsteps, I went to college and applied to medical school. Happenstance (and getting married and having a baby) brought me to retail. It was my perfect destiny.

$2.5 million, three stores, fifteen years. I absolutely loved it. I learned a lot. I've spent the next fifteen years using that knowledge and practical know-how to work with indie retailers to grow their stores, to love their numbers, and have a lot more fun.

My first retail job was a fluke. I agreed to work for a guy who I had met at a parenting class on condition that I could bring my daughter with me.

I discovered that I loved retail. I loved working with customers. I loved helping solve their problems and finding solutions to what they came in for. I found myself coming up with ideas for ways to increase sales and shared them with the owner.

The funny thing is, he didn't like any of my ideas. He made it clear that he didn't need any help.

One day as I was enthusiastically sharing a particularly powerful strategy (in my humble opinion), and passionately describing the long-lasting impact of it, he interrupted me and said, "If you have so many good ideas, you know what you should do? You should open your own store!"

I went home mulling it over – the sarcasm of his comment completely went over my head. I was still on the waiting list for medical school, so I thought, "I *will* open a store. How hard can it be?"

My favorite aunt had just died and given $10,000 to my sister and me. We went to a bank and the loan officer liked the fact that I had graduated from Notre Dame, and amazingly we got a loan for $100,000 with no other collateral.

Just like that, our store, Duck Duck Goose! opened for business. The concept was groundbreaking at the time. It was the first kids' lifestyle store. We combined clothing, accessories, toys, books, and gifts all under one roof. There was nothing else like it in the marketplace. We were successful immediately. It was wonderful! We were retail geniuses.

So what did we do? A mere nineteen months later, we opened another store. That is where our problems began. At first, everything went well and seemed on track. But then it all changed. The economy dipped and sales slowed. Oh my golly, it was really difficult. Nothing that had worked before was successful. We had no tools to use to change our results. We almost went bankrupt. *Twice.*

It was obvious that *something* had to change. A man walked into the store wearing a suit and carrying a briefcase. You can picture that scene. He might as well have had a blinking sign above his head saying, "I am a salesperson."

I was standing on a short ladder fixing an upper display. I was cranky. There was no cash flow. I certainly wasn't going to buy anything from this person who was obviously going to waste my time.

He approached me and asked the normal stupid salesperson questions. I didn't even meet his eyes as I tried to brush him off.

Then he asked me a question that got my attention.

"How is your cash flow?"

I whirled my head around. As I stood on the ladder, I remember thinking that my foot was the perfect height to hurt him very badly if I just kicked him. How dare he ask that question?

"It's horrible. Thank you very much." I replied.

"Would you like some help with it?" he asked.

That began a relationship that changed my life.

Marc Weiss from Management One helped us see the forest for the trees and taught us many things. Yes, we hired him. You see, I had no real retail experience. It just seemed like it shouldn't be that hard, right? That's what everybody says. But I wanted to *do better* and *know better* and *grow*.

With that knowledge, we got out of the hole we were in and opened up a third store. All together, we did well over *two and a half million dollars* of business in the three stores.

I was loving what I did, and loving the systems that I had put into place, and the freedom and lifestyle retail gave me. As I talked to other retailers that I met at trade shows, they weren't having the same results. I eagerly shared ideas that worked for us to help them improve their stores.

After a decade and a half of being a successful retailer, I realized that I loved helping others improve their businesses, and I wanted to share my knowledge and experience with other retailers full time. I sold my stores to do just that - to help retailers like you.

I founded RETAILMavens in 1999, so I could work with independent retailers, helping them have more profit and better results for more fun and better sleep. If you aren't having fun, then what's the point? Helping retailers enjoy their business - and their life again - is the cornerstone of my work.

At RETAILMavens, we help you develop a strong sense of identity - what sets you apart from the others - and put in place systems and strategies that make you love your business again. And you learn how to *never ignore your numbers*.

Before we get off and running, there are a couple of basic facts that you must know from the get-go.

You are not your numbers. So many people have judgment or think that there is judgment about what their numbers are. There's not. I love numbers because they are black and white, and they tell a story. They give me the tools I need to take my clients to another level, and to help them improve. That is all numbers are – a way of measuring where you are and of telling if your strategies are moving you in the right direction.

No one knows everything that they need to know. I have found that no one knows everything that they need to run a business. Every single independent retailer I work with has a different skill set. I work with some people who are incredibly good at advertising and marketing, but don't know how to manage their employees very well. Or someone who can manage his employees well has trouble with merchandising. You don't need to know everything. It's okay. Let yourself off the hook. Give yourself credit for wanting to learn more.

No more ignoring your numbers. Paying attention to your numbers is the most important thing you can do to have the success that you deserve and the lifestyle you want.

Chapter One
When you don't know what you don't know, you've failed before you've begun!

"To know what you know and what you do not know, that is true knowledge." Confucius

Doing the best you can is a stupid plan.

You wake up in the morning, yawn, and take a big stretch. Get up, dress, brush your teeth, and get ready to go to your store. On the drive in, you think, "Today is going to be a great day. I believe it. We are all going to do the best we can do today." You get out of the car and walk in the door.

What you don't know is that you have already failed.

You didn't need to get out of bed if that is your only plan for the day.

A positive attitude is helpful but it isn't enough for success. You MUST have a plan with specifics. Most often, those specifics include numbers.

"If you can't measure it, you can't improve it." ~Lord Kelvin

I would add to that by saying:

"If you don't know where you are, you don't know if you are improving or what to improve." ~Cathy Donovan Wagner

This is why doing your best is a waste of time. You must have determined precisely where you are, where you want to go and exactly what you need to do to improve to get there. *That* is what creates your plan. *That* is your key to success.

Retailers come to work with me because they have been trying to do their best —and it hasn't produced the results that they want – nor enough cash flow.

They have been without a plan and they ignore their numbers.

No one intends to run their business by the seat of their pants, but in the blink of an eye that is exactly what happens. It's a slippery slope. You keep trying harder and harder to make good decisions, but you don't know how or what to change. You keep sliding down. Faster and faster.

I know this story well. It happened to me. When my sister Patty and I opened our first store it was instantly successful. We were sure that we were retail geniuses and would be millionaires in no time. We had bought our new cars and were dreaming of vacation homes. Then we thought that if one was good, then two would be better. So right away we opened a second store.

When things are going well, the first thing people think of is being bigger, right? That isn't always the best idea. You won't be surprised to hear that along with indie stores, I love indie restaurants. No matter where I go, I always look for those local joints. I have favorite ones and I know you do, too.

I am sure we can all think of that great restaurant that you had to stand in line for and then they add on. Or add another location, because they all think that if one is good, two is better. And that isn't always true... mistakes and weaknesses come to light. The food isn't so great a couple of times and you stop going, right?

My favorite is a breakfast place called Benedicts. It has a tree growing right through the center of the building! The food is fabulous. They added another location and I went once and didn't have a great experience. I went back and was disappointed again. I didn't go back for a long while.

Our second store started out just fine. But it started to slip. Actually *we* started to slip....right down that slippery slope. Every successful action that we had taken for the first store *didn't work* in our second store.

We found ourselves working harder and harder...certain that persistence would solve the problem. We had no plan. We were flying by the seat of our pants. And the destination was surely disaster. Sales continued to drop, cash flow get tighter and tensions were high.

I found out that I was the best at doing the wrong things! The situation reminds me of that old line of when you find yourself in a hole you have to quit digging.

I called my godfather, Uncle Bill, to ask him for money. He looked at our numbers and said that he couldn't loan us anything.

"But why?" I asked. I had been certain that he would help.

"I am not sure that your store is viable," he answered.

What?

I offered all the typical excuses. "How do you know? You don't know retail." "My business is different than yours." You don't understand my store."

"You aren't paying attention to your numbers," he stated.

That was horrifically hard to hear. I was shocked. I hadn't realized how much I counted on being bailed out. Now we knew that it wasn't going to happen. The responsibility was all on us.

I was mad. I did know numbers. I love numbers! How dare he say that? But now, I see how it isn't just enough to know some numbers. Maybe you know what your rent is or your payroll usually runs. That's not the same as really knowing your numbers.

You may be saying to yourself, "Cathy, this is so elementary. How can you be in business and not know your numbers?"

The challenge is knowing the right numbers. We didn't.

Now I know I should have hugged Uncle Bill for turning me down. I thank him every day because I dedicated my life to helping other people know their numbers.

It took an expert to throw us a lifeline. We couldn't see for ourselves how to get off that slippery slope. That was when we learned how doing our best was never going to work. We needed a plan.

The only plan that would work was one that included knowledge of where we were, where we wanted to go, and how to get there. That plan had to include numbers so that we could measure our progress and success.

We knew that we did have numbers to look at, but we had no idea WHICH ones to look at. We didn't know what was good. We needed an education and an outside perspective on what to do and what to change.

My clients now are often in the same boat. They have great skills in some areas, and they work hard, but they simply don't know what they don't know. Some come to us when they are feeling the panic like I did back then, and some come to us to prevent being in that situation.

With my private clients, I give them a customized analysis of where they are right now. I talk to them about their dreams and what is possible. Then I work out a plan with them to get them where they want to go. We're going to work together in this book to give you some of the same tools and help you get the success you deserve.

Before we jump in, I want to clear up some common misunderstandings.

Cash Flow Does Not Equal Profit

Probably the most common misunderstanding: Cash flow does not equal profit.

A store can be profitable and still go bankrupt from cash flow problems. It happens all the time.

Cash flow is the money that flows in and out of the store. It is essential to the success of the store...and to your personal happiness and a good night's sleep.

Profit is what is left over from your sales after all of your expenses have been deducted. It is what you get to keep in your pocket. The biggest difference between cash flow and profit is the difference between success and bankruptcy.

How many times have you looked at your financials and felt like they must belong to a different store?! I remember going to see my accountant during our tough times.

"Good news, Cathy! You made a profit last year," the accountant said.

"What?" I cried as I fell into the chair in his office. "But I have no money!" A profit simply didn't seem possible. There was NO money in the bank account.

Get that straight: profit does not equal cash flow.

What Are Financials?

Next, let's be sure that you are crystal clear about what financials are. If you aren't sure, know that you are in good company. Many retailers don't but are afraid to ask. I once was.

After placing an order with a new vendor, they called about payment terms.

"I want net 30 terms," I stated.

"Alright," the vendor replied, "but I will need to review your financials for the last two years."

"That sounds fine," I said as I hung up the phone.

I slumped in my chair with a sick feeling in the pit of my stomach because I didn't know what they were asking for. Now I don't mind acknowledging that I don't know something and asking a question. But the problem here is that I KNEW I SHOULD KNOW. EVERY good businessperson does.

I was spending and generating hundreds of thousands of dollars – didn't that make me a good businessperson?! The answer to that question is NO.

My sales volume had nothing to do with my financial knowledge. But I was right to feel nauseous. And I decided that I had to take control and get an education about this…just like you are today. Congratulations.

Financials are composed of two documents: Balance Sheet and Profit and Loss (aka Income Statement). These documents are simply a picture of a financial moment in time…like the amount that you weigh. If I ask you that, it can bring up an emotional response, right?

Don't let that happen with financials. They are just what your situation was on that particular day. They are most valuable in context of where you were last year.

For example, I looked at my weight this morning and did a double take. It was higher than I thought it should be. Then I remembered that I had Chinese for dinner last night, which means that I was retaining water. Knowing that provides the context for the number that was the amount that I weighed. If my number was twenty pounds more than a year ago, then it's time to take notice.

A Break Even Analysis is Pointless

"Hi Cathy, I want to hire you to help me break even."

No one hires me for that! Do you want to just break even? Well, maybe you just keep on doing what you're doing.

Seriously, you need to know your profit point. You need to know your numbers. Are you ready to roll up your sleeves and get to work?

Want to hear a ridiculous fact? Many retailers don't know the amount of sales that they need in order to cover all expenses and pay themselves.

That information is often referred to as a break even analysis —and that is a completely ridiculous document.

Who wants to just break even?

I create for my clients a Profit Point and Opportunity Analysis because that is what I want for you! You must know your profit point – which includes ALL your expenses and your salary and your debt payments. Doesn't profit sound better than break even?

When you have that put together you can then analyze your opportunities. Once you know where you are, you can see what can be changed.

You can get from here to there if you don't even know where "here" is.

Calculate Your Profit Point

Start by getting your financials together for the last two years. I want you to do your Profit Point for both of those years so that you can see how the numbers compare and see if they have increased or decreased.

I'm also going to make sure that we're absolutely clear about all the definitions here.

Put in your sales after returns and without sales tax. Don't include sales tax because it's not money that belongs to us so we don't count it. It is money that just flows through; it goes in and it goes out.

COGS stands for the cost of goods sold and that's done without freight. Freight is not included here for our purposes because it is an expense.

You can only control the amount of money you spend on inventory. We look at freight to be a percentage of what your COGS is.

Next, enter payroll without your payroll taxes. It includes everyone. I've often seen a situation where a store will have somebody who helps in the back and they don't include them. Oh no, this number has to include everyone that works on the floor or with the inventory. It doesn't include people who don't work on the floor and only provide accounting services, cleaning services, merchandising services or advertising services.

When you enter rent, be sure to include taxes and CAM (common area maintenance) and anything else that you pay to your landlord.

Are you with me so far?

Let's make sure that we are clear on advertising and marketing. This number includes everything that you do that is part of advertising and marketing. All expenses of an event are included; if you do a Girl's Night Out, it includes all the drinks and food that you serve. The only exception is if you sell those items in your store. Then, mark the items used down to zero and report them as a mark down; they don't count in this expense.

If you mail out birthday cards, the printing and postage is included here. Sometimes in a mall, you have a situation where you have to pay advertising and marketing to your landlord. In that case, I take it out of the rent and include it in advertising and marketing.

We are wanting to have an accurate look at what numbers are what.

Finally, add all the other expenses from your profit and loss statement together.

There's one very important point that is often missed: there are expenses listed on your balance sheet. There are monthly payments made for assets or liabilities that are reflected on your balance sheet. These are missed and you are screwed.

They are payments that you make monthly. Many are debt payments; paying down your bank loan, paying down your home equity loan or if you have a line of credit for your home. Any payments like that are listed on your balance sheet because when you make a payment, the amount that shows as being due is decreased. That's why they call it a balance sheet expense. It also includes monthly payments to pay down a credit card balance that is outstanding.

It can get slightly confusing so I want to make sure that we're making this crystal clear. Any monthly payments you make have to be included. I mentioned loan and credit card payments, but maybe you bought a car through the store and you have a monthly car payment; that would go also under debt payments.

The insurance and all other car expenses are listed as expenses on your Profit and Loss. Every once in a while I'll find someone who's bought a point of sale system and they're making a monthly payment on that. So any sort of monthly payments are included with that debt payment amount. This is a critical part that many people don't get.

Once you have all those numbers, then what I want you to do is add them up. Add up the cost of goods, your payroll, your rent, your advertising/marketing, and then all those other expenses and your debt payments. The total of all of those together is the amount of sales that you must start at to generate more profit and more positive cash flow.

That is your profit point.

Isn't that exciting? It's exhilarating to be able to know definitively where you move from breaking even into profit.

Now, the key is to look at what your last year's sales were and subtract out your profit point.

It's this number that's going to tell us the truth.

Your Profit Point

Add together the following numbers:

_____ COGS (Cost of Goods Sold without freight)

+ _____ Payroll (without taxes, including yourself)

+ _____ Rent (including taxes and CAM)

+ _____ Advertising/Marketing (everything related to it)

+ _____ All Other Expenses & Debt Payments

= _____ **THIS IS THE AMOUNT OF SALES YOU MUST START AT TO GENERATE PROFIT AND MORE POSITIVE CASH FLOW**

RETAIL*Mavens*

(Now you see why I wanted you to get two years of numbers.)

Okay, subtract the profit point from last year's sales.

If it's a positive number you can do the money dance, woohoo!

If it's a negative number, we're just going to roll up our sleeves and take control of our numbers. Do not despair. Don't judge yourself. No negative self-talk.

Have you been an ostrich? Sticking your head in the sand and avoiding this? You may have been ignoring your numbers and you are not alone. We are going to change that. The problem with being an ostrich is that you end up leaving your back end out and up high as a great target to get spanked. I want you to be an ostrich proudly strutting around with those beautiful feathers. No matter what the number is, you know it now and can address it.

The Moment of Truth

_____ Last Year's Sales

– (less) _____ Profit Point

= (equals) _____

Is it...

A positive number? *Do the money dance!*

A negative number? *Roll up your sleeves!*

RETAIL *Mavens*

Let me remind you that just by being here with me in this book, you've committed to learning more, to getting better results. Also let me tell you that I can count on one hand the number of retailers I've met who have even done this exercise. You've done it now. I'm proud of you. Way to go. Now there's so much for us to do.

Profit Point Example:

  $287,000 **COGS** (Cost of Goods Sold without freight)

+ $124,000 **Payroll** (without taxes including yourself)

+ $ 52,000 **Rent** (including taxes and CAM)

+ $ 17,000 **Advertising/Marketing** (ALL related to it)

+ <u>$ 36,000</u> **All Other Expenses + Debt Payments**

  $516,000   THIS IS THE AMOUNT OF SALES YOU MUST
                      START AT TO GENERATE MORE PROFIT
                      AND MORE POSITIVE CASH FLOW

Let's walk through an example. Let's say the figures used here are your real numbers. You totaled your cost of goods, your payroll, your rent, your advertising and marketing, and all of your other expenses and your debt payments. Your total amount is $516,000.

$516,000 is the amount of sales you've got to start at in order to generate profit and have a positive cash flow.

This is the moment of truth. You need to look at last year's sales. Let's say they were $500,000. Subtract your total above from last year's sales.

$500,000 - $516,000.

Your profit point is $516,000; that means that you were short $16,000.

Like I said, no big deal, no judgment, it just is what it is and now you know to fix it. Numbers tell us the story of what needs to be fixed.

Let's do some fixing.

Assignment:

1. Calculate your store's profit point! Use the forms above.

2. Do the money dance, or roll up those sleeves! Remember, you are not your numbers. They are a snapshot in time that will show us the way forward.

Chapter Two
Don't play hide and seek with your profits

"Mistakes are the usual bridge between inexperience and wisdom." Phyllis Theroux

Time and time again, I see the two biggest problems retailers make.

The biggest problem is usually that the cost of goods is too high. Retailers spend too much on inventory and wait too long for it to sell.

You are actually walking over thousands and thousands of dollars on your sales floor that should not be on there. Those dollars should be in your pocket!

The Tale of The Christmas Urn

Let me tell you a story about this exact thing. Emily opened her garden and gift store sixteen years ago. When she talked about her store, you could hear both the excitement and frustration in her voice. Her sales volume was just over $300,000 and she had about $275,000 in inventory at retail on her floor.

Emily told me, "I love what I do but just can't seem to get cash flow going."

"Emily, you bought way too much inventory – you have to move $100,000 of that out!" I told her. "*That* is why you are having cash flow problems."

Many retailers balk when I tell them they have to move some inventory quickly. I've been working with stores for fifteen years and I know *all* the stories. I even told them myself when I had my own stores for a decade and a half.

Emily told me the story of the urn. "You know Cathy, sales just don't ever work. You have to just wait for the right person to walk through the door. Why, I had this lovely turquoise urn and I marked it down for sales and it would never move. So I would mark it back up. Then next sidewalk sale, I would mark it down again but no one even looked at it. Then last Christmas Eve, a woman came in and squealed with delight when she saw it. She said her sister would love it. She was my last sale of the Christmas season and I was so happy that the urn was going to a good home."

"What was the price of it?" I asked, thinking that perhaps it was very expensive and that was why it hadn't sold.

"It was $40. And I marked it down as far as $25 but it never moved."

So, the price wasn't why it hadn't moved.

"How long had you had that urn, Emily?

I could hear her fingertips tapping on her POS keyboard as she said, "Just a second, let me check. I got it in the year....2000...."

There was a pause.

"Cathy, are you still there?"

"Oh yes, Emily, I was just waiting to hear when you received the urn."

"I already told you. It was in the year 2000."

WHAT? I was speechless. I wanted to suggest that she should have increased the price because now the item was surely an antique.

She didn't realize the crucial mistake she made. And she was complaining about cash flow when there was cash all around her.

Think about it. She had bought that urn for $20 almost 15 years ago. There was a $20 bill sitting on her sales floor that she walked past many times each and every day. She didn't know the science that she could have put to use to move the urn out and put cash into her pocket. I go over the science in great detail in our RETAILMavens Killer Clearance Sale Secrets toolkit. Let me clue you in some right now.

Common Mistakes

There are two common mistakes made all the time.

One of our RETAILMavens first laws is that NO ITEM CAN CELEBRATE A BIRTHDAY. Period. You must move it out. No matter what. Retailers will wait for that "perfect person." Retailers make the mistake of hanging on when they should be letting go.

This leads to the 2nd law. KEEP MARKING DOWN TO KEEP THE CASH FLOWING

Retailers get it into their head that they are losing their shirts if they mark an item down to a price below what they paid for it.

That is NOT seeing the big picture. Emily made that mistake. She paid $20 for the urn and told me that she had marked it down "as far as $25!"

Obviously that was a big discount for her. But it was crazy and she lost so much more money because she didn't take more markdowns.

Let me tell you how the story of the Christmas Urn should have gone.

The urn is put out and prominently displayed. It doesn't sell. It is moved around to different areas in the store. At one point it is highlighted on the front counter. Another time it is placed in the front window. It still doesn't sell.

The urn is marked down 25% off and now is $30. There is still no interest in it. Next we mark it down to 50% off. Yet, even at the incredibly low price of $20, still the urn doesn't sell.

Finally, the urn is taken to the last markdown of 75% off which means it is now priced at $10. As painful as that may seem, you simply have to get over it your emotions. It doesn't matter that you think it is worth more than that. No one else does. And if you don't move items, you can't buy new ones. If you don't buy new merchandise, people will stop coming in because they are tired of seeing the same things over and over. So traffic and sales slow down even more.

Wait until you see what is about to happen.

At last, a savvy shopper brings it to the counter, hands Emily $10 and brings the urn home. Hooray! Emily has $10 in her hand. She takes that money and buys a vase that she can retail at $20. That vase sells quickly and Emily now has $20.

Now, Emily decides to buy 2 more of that popular vase. One sells immediately for $20 but the other doesn't move until it is marked down to $5, which is 75% off. She took that quick action because she wanted more cash to buy more of those hot vases that were blowing out.

Can you see all the cash flow that happened because Emily marked that urn down? She took that $10 and generated 3 more sales from it. The key is that she kept the markdowns going and kept the cash flowing.

Don't miss the other strategy that I shared in that story. Notice that I had her take specific graduated markdowns. That always works best to move out the item and allows you to keep more profit than any other way.

(To get more secrets, check out Killer Clearance Sales Secrets at www.retailmavens.com.)

The second biggest mistake retailers make is ignoring what their raving fans are telling them.

Now why would you do that? Your raving fans vote with their dollars and tell you what they want you to carry more of. Not enough attention is paid to your best sellers. I know; I made this mistake too.

I was talking to a first time grandma about this wonderful wood rattle that my 6-month-old son just loved. It kept him occupied and happy for so long.

"I'll take it," she said.

As I walked to the spot where it hung, I started to wonder if we had them in stock. I got a sinking feeling in my stomach as I realized I couldn't remember if I had reordered them. Sure enough, the spot was EMPTY. I was out of that best seller. I wanted to scream, "NOO!"

How many times has that happened to you too? That is when I created my N.O.O. list – which stands for Never Out Of. (To get a N.O.O. LIST, go to www.retailmavens.com/noo.)

Purposefully, identify your best sellers in your store using your POS system and your team for resources. Then give the job to someone else.

You know what other people want to buy. Right? You have that fabulous new jean or great wrap bracelet or that fantastic floral scarf. Now imagine a customer comes in, walks up to you and tells you how they love that scarf that they bought from you a bit ago. Now they want one for their friend and you say with a big smile on your face, "Sure, let's go pick one out. They are right over here."

As you start walking to it, you are thinking "I so hope I have another one, I so hope I have another...." And then you look at a hole on the shelf. NOO!

We hate when that happens. It is hard to stay on top of all the items that move fast. Yet, you are throwing away dollars if you don't find a way to do so.

The trick is to create your N.O.O. (Never Out Of) List. I can tell you precisely how to do this and how to follow-through with it – effortlessly and easily.

First, what goes on the list? Start with the 20 items that you sold the most units of in the last 12 months.... and lay that against the list of the items that you sold the most of last November and December because sometimes that can be different.

List these down on a sheet of paper and make 11 columns next to them.

In the first box next to each item write down how many you sell in a 1-month period. Presto. You have now set your minimum inventory requirement. That is the title of your first column.

Above the next cell write DATE and in the next write INV OH, which stands for inventory on hand.

You will track what your current inventory level is for every two weeks starting with today.

This takes us to my favorite part – the effortless part. You ARE NOT to count it. Because let's be honest – you have too much else to do. Give it to your most reliable person. They are to fill this report out each week with the date and the quantity and put it on your desk. (RETAILMavens Tip – this is the kind of detail that we love to help you with. Use neon colored paper and a clipboard.)

Download a sample form at www.retailmavens.com/noo.

Now you place reorders for the items that your customers have voted that they love the most. That's how we look at it – every time a customer makes a purchase they are placing a vote with their dollars.

They tell you what they want you to carry. This is a great way of making sure that you are giving them what they want.

Every single time we have clients do this exercise, they find items that they are out of stock on. They have lost business because of it.

Want to take this tactic to the next level?

Not everyone will and they will miss out on cash that their fans can't wait to give them.

This is our RETAILMavens Go Big or Go Home strategy. It creates hyper focus on your key items. Determine 2-3 items that would appeal to different categories of your raving fans and are at a price point that is higher than your average sale.

Go really deep in them and order 2 times what you would normally order. Commit to an amount that scares you.

Then commit to sell them.

It is that simple. It always works.

Merchandise them by putting them in a big stack and wrap some up as beautiful gifts. Put some on a table right by the front counter. As you walk up to ring your customer up, you can say, "Hey, have you seen this...." Completely train your team on the features and benefits of the items. We want your team to have the selling benefits committed to memory because you are all committed to selling all you have.

Once you sell out, move on to the next item. Always have a Go Big or Go Home item being sold in your store. It builds confidence in your team as they sell more expensive items easily.

It also opens your eyes to what else it is that your raving fans will buy.

Assignment:

1. Move the dogs – anything over a year old, make a plan to move it out. Write down 5 items that you know you have to move now.

2. Create your stores N.O.O. list and assign it to a team member! Who is going to be responsible for doing it for you?

3. Choose a Go Big or Go Home item and sell it! What will it be?

Chapter Three
Mark it up, mark it down, move it out:
The art and science of pricing like a pro

*"All I ask is the chance to prove that money
can't make me happy." –Spike Milligan*

Retailers usually pay attention to their sales numbers.

You can ask someone how their business is going and their response is about how their sales compared to last year. That is an important number to know, but…

Retailers are ignoring one of the most important numbers. It has a huge impact on their profits and on the cash that they bring home.

My favorite story about this is the client that fought me for years about it. Finally, she agreed to try it. Sales went up. And she used the extra cash to take her family on a cruise in the Bahamas – their first family vacation in over five years.

What number is this?

It is your initial markup - IMU. It is the difference between what you're bringing in at cost and then how much you're marking it up. In that difference is your increased cash, cash flow and profit. Measuring your initial markup is essential.

You can't just guess what it is; you've got to measure it. Why? You have to know what the total IMU is for last 12 months because of all the impact it has on your store.

It creates a cushion for markdowns.

It generates additional revenue.

It absolutely generates additional profits for you, and it provides *the money you can keep in your pocket*.

It is the simple equation of the retail price minus the cost price divided by the retail price and then that number multiplied by 100.

IMU= [(Retail price – Cost price)/Retail price] X 100

Almost all retailers miss it and they certainly don't understand it. So are you interested in creating more cash and creating more profit? I thought so. So stick with me. You must increase your initial mark up which means increasing your prices.

I know what you are thinking.

"I can't increase my prices."

"Everyone checks the internet for pricing."

"You surely don't understand my customers. They will all complain and all stop shopping."

Do not shut down here or you will miss an incredible opportunity. Every single private client I have ever worked with has thought they couldn't do this. When I give a talk and share this strategy, retailers just start shaking their heads.

In fact I felt the same way at first too! But I was desperate for more cash and willing to try anything. It worked. And our sales increased. Of course, some people complained but our business kept growing, proving that people kept shopping with us.

In the over fifteen years that I have been working with private clients, this is the very first thing I tell them to so. It always works. 100% of the time it is successful.

Yes, you can increase your prices. You deserve it. Margins are so slim in retail and this extra percentage will make all the difference in the world to your bottom line.

A key point to understand is that I am referring to your TOTAL initial markup. Over 12 months, your initial markup must equal 55% at least. (This is for most stores. Don't hesitate to go to www.facebook.com/retailmavens and ask me about your type of store specifically.)

Every store has some items that they can't take a higher mark up on. A common example is that often books and publications come pre-priced so there is no option there. Often bigger items from well-known vendors can't be marked up further because they are compared all around.

Your job is to find items that CAN be marked up. Save 10% of your open to buy (your budgeted inventory amount) to spend on inventory that you can mark up even more. (To be clear, your open to buy – OTB – is your budgeted amount to spend on inventory)

Look for smaller accessory items that cost $5 and mark them to $15. That is where much of the extra markup can come from.

Now let's look at how initial markup creates cash.

IMU - Creates Cash

Consider 2 stores that both spend
$500,000 per year on inventory

Ashley: Takes a 50% IMU
that equals $1,000,000 at Retail

Dave: Takes a 55% IMU
that equals $1,111,111 at Retail

That is a **$111,111**
increase in cash flow

RETAIL *Mavens*

Consider two stores that both spend $500,000 per year in inventory. Ashley takes a 50 percent initial markup, so that means that her $500,000 becomes a million dollars at retail.

Dave on the other hand takes a 55 percent initial markup, which means that that $500,000 for him becomes $1,111,111 at retail. That is an increase of over $111,000.

So I'm just asking, who would you want to be? Ashley or Dave? I thought so.

Dave saw that $111,111 increase in cash flow, and only by increasing his initial markup by 5 percent. Do you know what the difference of that means? The difference is simply multiplying by 2.2 instead of multiplying by 2.

That's all it takes.

$1 M V$ - Creates Cash

Dave sees
$111,111
increase in cash flow

* Only 5% increase in IMU!
*Multiplying the cost by 2.2 instead of 2!
*Every transaction equals greater revenue

RETAIL *Mavens*

It's incredible the difference it makes. Just a tiny little percentage of difference and that can make the difference in cash flow.

In addition, every single transaction then also equals greater revenue. That is a sweet thing.

Let's look at how initial markup can create profit.

Consider two stores that are doing the same sales volume of $500,000 and they're taking the same percentage of annual markdowns, 20 percent. So what that means is that they look at how much they mark down in total dollars and they divide it by their total sales volume. That's how they come up with the 20 percent total markdowns.

Heather set her initial markup at 50 percent, and that makes her maintained markup (or her gross profit which is the money from sales after you pay for inventory) equal to 37.5. Okay.

Let me tell you how you define that. You have your initial markup, which means that she takes a ball that's $10 and marks it up to $20. Then because she takes markdowns, her maintained markup which then is the amount of gross profit that remains after taking into account markdown, that number equals 37.5. For every $100 that she brings in, $37.50 goes towards profit.

Terri on the other hand set her initial markup at 55 percent. Therefore, her maintained markup is 44 percent. So you might look at those numbers and think that's 6.5 percent difference. It's just a small number. What's the big deal?

IMU - Creates Profit

Consider 2 stores doing the same sales volume – **$500,000**, and taking the same percentage of annual markdowns – **20%**

Heather: set her IMU at 50%, which makes her MMU (gross profit) equal to 37.5%

Terri: set her IMU at 55%, which makes her MMU (gross profit) equal to 44%

Only 6.5% difference...a small number

RETAIL*Mavens*

Take the annual sales of $500,000 and multiply that by 6.5%, which equals $32,500. That 6.5 percent difference represents an additional $32,500 that Terri can put in her pocket because she took more of an initial markup.

An extra $32,500. Want some of that?

**Earn your RETAILMavens Price-Point PhD:
The Psychology of Pricing for Profit**

Another trick that works magic...The Psychology of Pricing For More Profit.

In my years as an indie specialty retailer, I got pricing down to a science. I didn't know at the time that it actually IS a science. Behavioral economics and the study of psychology of retail shoppers is fascinating.

What a person will pay is based on their perception of the value of the item.

I learned in my store that adding a couple of dollars here and there didn't change the customer's perception of the value. An item that is $8 can be sold for $10. Now look at an item that is $21. It should be priced at $22. That price just looks better, doesn't it? And you would still buy it, right? Adding that dollar or two has a HUGE impact on your profit.

That is how you can achieve a minimum of a 55% initial markup (IMU) for your store.

The easiest way to get that is to look at your inventory and see where you can use the pricing guidelines below. You will find it easier than you think.

My new clients fight me tooth and nail about this, and then see how easy it is to mark up SOME items a little more. They become eager to do it as they see that impact is profound. And sales don't drop.

For a store doing $500,000, increasing your IMU from 50% to 55% can give you an additional $25,000 in potential cash flow!

ORIGINAL PRICE	PROFIT PRICING	NOTES
0 - $3.00	Use only the .50 or the .00	Don't bother pricing with the .25 or .75 as it won't make a difference and people will pay more without a thought.
$4.00 - $5.00	$5.00	A customer considers a $4 item to really be a $5 item anyway.
$6.00 - $8.00	$8.00	Use only when you have to – think hard and consider if the value of the item is really $10. I bet it is.
$9.00 - $10.00	$10.00	In their heads, a customer considers it a $10 item anyway.
$11.00 - $12.00	$12.00	An $11.00 looks like it should have been $10. I recommend not even using this and just going straight to $15.
$13.00 - $15.00	$15.00	People like to think in 5's. If it is $13 or $14, it might as well be $15.
$16.00 - $18.00	$18.00	I recommend not even using this and just going straight to $20.
$19.00 - $20.00	$20.00	As the prices get higher, I find that the extra dollar or two or three won't stop a customer from buying it.
$21.00 - $22.00	$22.00	Keep the extra few dollars for yourself.
$23.00 - $25.00	$25	No discernible difference for the customers.
Above $25.00	Increase by $5 up to $100	
Above $100	Increase by $25.	Try it. Really look at an item. No one will buy an item at $140 that they wouldn't buy at $150.

These are the only prices that you should use in your store.

Assignment:

1. Look for 10 items in your store that you can take a larger
   initial markup on using the 2.2 multiplier. Don't stop until
   you have 10. Name them here.

2. Examine your pricing and adjust it based on what you now
   know of the psychology of retail pricing. Set a deadline for
   yourself right here.

3. Copy the pricing guide above or go to
   www.retailmavens.com/pricing and print a guide.

Chapter Four

Taming the Inventory Beast:
Eating the Proverbial Elephant One Bite at a Time

Start by doing what's necessary; then do what's possible; and suddenly you are doing the impossible. –Francis of Assisi

You want steady cash flow and a larger paycheck. You want your sales and profits to grow. The most important step that you can take is to manage your single largest expense well.

The destination for your store is growth, right? That means that you have to learn how to better control your inventory.

The effort that you spend doing that yields a large impact because cost of goods represents about 50% of your sales on your profit and loss.

Stop for a moment and really think about that. If you do $400,000 in business, you are spending about $200,000 on your inventory in a year.

If you were buying one item that cost that much - $200,000, think about how much research and effort you would put into making a good decision.

You would spend *hours* online looking at all the different options. You might even buy reports full of information to help you. You would ask the advice of others.

Yet, as buyers, aren't we all guilty of spending $500 here and $1200 and $2500 there without knowing for sure if it is being spent where it should be? In the blink of an eye, we have spent $200,000 or the price of a vacation home. That shouldn't happen.

As a client told me, "I'm tired of feeling like I'm not doing everything I can to be successful." Take control of your inventory and grow.

How to better control your inventory? One bite at a time. One step at a time. One class at a time. Let me begin to school you.

You have to look at the thousands of SKUs in your store and group them into classifications of inventory – or classes. A class is a group of similar inventory; similar in type of play and inventory turn.

By breaking your inventory down into manageable bite size pieces, it is easy to control. When you look at your store by classes, you can analyze sales and inventory levels better. And when that happens, it becomes easier to control. The result is increased growth in your sales and profits.

We all want to give customers what they want. Our customers tell us what they want every time that they buy something from us. They are voting with each dollar they spend. When you have classes, you can track what they want from you and make sure that you have just enough for them. That knowledge gives you power.

Now, you can take action on the basis of the knowledge of what the demand is for the class. Let's say that you want to increase your purchases for the holiday by 10% because you believe that your business will grow that much. Just adding 10% across the board would be a big mistake. Business never grows evenly in every class.

What happens is that some classes will be up 20%, maybe even 25%, while some will be down 15%. If you just added 10% to all your orders, you would end up over inventoried in some classes and under inventoried in others. You would be sending your clients away to shop elsewhere because you couldn't give them what they wanted.

When you know the demand of each class, you can look at how each is trending and then buy accordingly.

How We Beat Industry Benchmarks!

Let's use toy stores as an example. In the decades that I have worked with toy stores, I have come up with a good class structure. There are enough classes to get good data and not too many so that it is unmanageable. In the next column, I share what a good percentage breakdown of sales is for the classes.

CLASS NAME	% of Annual Sales	Profit Grade
Arts and Crafts	11	A+
Books and Music	8	
Building	6	F
Dolls	3	
Games	10	
Gifts	7	F
Infant	9	
Niddlies/Impulse	8	A+
Pretend Play	5	
Outdoor	10	
Plush	7	
Science/Eductn.	6	
Transportation	7	
Puzzles	3	

There is hidden treasure in the table above.

I compare my clients' annual sales percentages to these and I look for opportunities for growth. Every store has its own particular area of expertise, and sales in a certain class will show that by being much higher than this average. That is great and I wouldn't have them change a thing in those classes.

There are always two or three classes that are less than average. Right away, I start talking to the owner about how to grow those areas. What do they carry? Have they checked with listserv to see what are the hottest items in those classes for other stores?

This is a proven way to increase sales right away. That's the hidden treasure that they didn't even know was right beneath their nose.

The last column shows the profit grade of the class. It is only meant for general guidance – don't over react to it.

The profit grade is determined by the gross margin return of investment (GMROI) for those classes. The GMROI is basically the report card for how much money a class makes for you. Two classes – Arts & Crafts and Niddlies/Impulse Items – are usually the most profitable classes over all.

I included that information to show you where you can take more risks in choosing inventory. I encourage clients to try new items in those classes because the extra profit can make up for markdowns that you might have to take if those new items don't sell.

On the other hand, be more cautious with Building. I find that many stores have their favorite Building toys – and usually they are the favorite of the owner or salespeople. Don't hesitate to search for a new Building toy to fall in love with! Just take time to play with it and be sure that everyone feels the same way you do about it.

The class of Gifts is only unprofitable because it usually ends up being the miscellaneous class. Items that don't fit into other classes go in here – and often those are items that shouldn't have been bought for the store in the first place.

You have to make sure that you take an extra markup on items in this class and then mark them down quickly if they don't start selling quickly. One area in this class that is a source of hidden treasure is kids' jewelry. Usually, this sells very well for toy stores and it isn't always considered.

One of the toy trade groups offers an industry wide financial analysis report. Every one of my toy store clients has blown away the 'High Profit' stores in that report. They are all much more profitable than the numbers in that report show is possible! That is because of the analysis that we do with them on a class by class basis.

If you want the same results for your store, send an email to clientcare@retailmavens.com and we will arrange a conversation.

For All Other Industries

We apply these same ideas to all of the stores that we work with. We work with every kind of retailer under the sun.

Every retail store has money coming in the front door from customers and going out the back door to vendors and landlords and more. The common problem is that there isn't enough money left over in the owner's pocket. Although the merchandise sold is different, the science of this works for every store.

This concept of looking at your inventory by classes will help you start growing. It will get you going towards getting better control of your inventory.

Assignment:

1. Sort your inventory into 10 to 15 classifications.

2. Which classes are working for you?

3. Which classes need work?

Chapter Five
Turn up your turn! Master the most misunderstood retail science and maximize your cash flow.

"The fact is that one of the earliest lessons I learned in business was that balance sheets and income statements are fiction, cash flow is reality." Chris Chocola

Turn puts dollars into my pocket…plain and simple.

It seems like it was only yesterday…the day that I remember REALLY understanding the concept of turn and how closely it impacts my profits.

Since that day, I have explained it to hundreds of other retailers. It is one of the most talked about and most misunderstood topics of retail conversation.

By definition, turn is the number of times each year the inventory in your store sells through. It is the number of times in a year that your store is completely cleared out of old inventory and filled with new.

The higher the number of turns you get, the better it is for your bank balance. Every time you sell an item, you recoup its cost and earn the profit you need to pay yourself and all your other expenses.

How to figure it out? There are two essential components to keep in mind. First, turn is determined over 13 months; it is more about the whole journey that it is about one three-month selling season. You must include 13 months to account for seasonal swings in inventory.

Second, always remember that turn is nothing more than a fraction.

$$\text{Turn} = \frac{\text{Annual Sales (at retail without sales tax)}}{\text{Average Inventory (at retail) for 13 months}}$$

You can increase turn two ways. Remember, it is just a fraction: numerator/denominator. You divide your annual sales by average inventory (13 months).

Let's play with the numbers to increase turn. The first is to decrease your average inventory (the denominator of the fraction). Using a math equation as an example, if 6/6 =1, and we wanted to increase the 1, we would keep less inventory – 6/2 = 3.

The second way is to keep the same inventory but increase sales (the numerator) – 18/6 = 3.

If you have a turn rate of 3 times per year how long does that mean merchandise is sitting on your shelves?

We determine that by dividing the number of weeks in a year – 52 – by the desired number of turns in a year – 3. So 52 weeks divided by 3 turns is 18 weeks on a shelf.

This is a great tool to use to determine what items to markdown at what time. If you are aiming for a 3 time turn in your store then items shouldn't be sitting around for longer than 18 weeks.

If an item is in your store for too long, it is turning too slow and not making the money it should for you. On the other hand, if you are constantly out of an item, it is turning too fast. You are missing opportunities for sales and thus losing money.

Your goal is to find a balance and maximize the flow of cash for your store.

Stephanie was a client who owned a wonderful women's clothing store and carried a fantastic selection of jewelry. We wanted to grow her business and increase her cash flow. So, we were looking for hidden opportunities within her classes.

The turn of every store is determined by the sum of its classes. Each class or group of merchandise has a different turn. Each type of store has a different combination of classes, so they all have a different optimal turn rate.

Apparel stores turn the fastest – many as high as 4 times per year. Gift stores are at about 2.5. Women's stores that carry apparel *and* jewelry should consider the two separately. A good turn for apparel is 3.5 and jewelry turn more frequently at about 3.7

When I first start to work with a store, I find that the vast majority are turning much too slow. If you are unsure of where to start, aim at turn rate of 3 times a year. Don't hesitate to ask me what the general guideline should be for your store at www.facebook.com/retailmavens.

Turn is directly related to the stock-to-sales ratio that can help to explain this more clearly. The stock-to-sales ratio is about how much stock or variety of items a customer needs to evaluate before they make a decision to buy.

Due to the quantity of choices necessary, a customer that is purchasing an article of clothing requires *more* merchandise to analyze before they purchase on item. Take for example, a woman that needs a new pair of colored denim jeans. What size? What color? What fit? There are so many options to consider.

That customer needs to see more items before she can buy just one pair of jeans. Often as many as 5 or 6 pairs of jeans must be evaluated before she picks one. So much more inventory is required of jeans. You can see how that slows down the turn. Conversely I know that a woman needs to look at fewer items of jewelry to buy one piece.

Now this client's jewelry business was already divided into classes that allowed us to analyze it. Necklaces had generated $79,752 in the last year with a turn of 3.1. In discussing this class we realized that it really had two sides to it: brand name products and cheaper no name products.

I had Stephanie split them apart so we could really see how each side did and give them each a chance to grow. It is all about identifying opportunities. The brand name skus had done $45,289 while the cheaper no name items had generated $34,463 in sales

First, we looked at the brand name side and slowed down the turn slightly to 2.7. By doing this, we gave the customers more selection, which was important because the price points were higher.

We took her sales for the year and divided it by that number to see what her average inventory should be. (Hint: $45,289/2.7= $16,774 Keep in mind that this is the amount of inventory at retail.)

When using that average inventory amount, be sure to build it up before the bigger sales volume months. You must watch this monthly. By doing this, we gave the customers more selection, which was important because the price points were higher.

Another great strategy to increase sales is identify the key best sellers and carry more of them in stock. We also educated the customer more about the brands she carried through increased signage and in her weekly emails.

I wanted the cheaper no name skus to generate more profit and set that turn rate to 3.7. I showed Stephanie that by speeding up her turn from 3.1 to 3.7 she would be able to put over $2000 into the bank without even increasing her sales which had been $29,000 for that new class.

$29,000 in sales	$29,000 in sales
3.1=$9,935 in average inventory	3.7=$7,838 in average inventory

She can maintain the same sales with $2,000 less inventory. Are you wondering how? I'm glad you asked!

I started by showing her how long an item can stay on her floor. By using our formula of 52 weeks in the year divided by 3.7 which is our desired turn rate, Stephanie knew she had to identify all items that had been on the floor longer than 14 weeks. Those dogs were marked down and moved out! Then she replaced them with faster selling goods.

By taking these actions and watching the performance every month, we had phenomenal results. At the end of that year, the brand name class did $77,921 and the other class did $18,880 for a combined total of $96,771 in sales.

In the previous year, jewelry total had done $79,752. This meant she had a 21% increase of $17,019. Most importantly, it meant that my client got an extra $9,718 profit!

That's how much extra money she has in the bank by paying attention to her turn. We love to find these hidden opportunities for our private clients.

Another Case Study About Turn

The following is a true story. The names have been changed to protect the innocent idiot.

Pat owned a toy and children's clothing store. After a great year in which she was up about $42,000 from the previous year, even while she maintained the same expense structure, Pat was looking forward to seeing her accountant. "There will be good news," she thought.

Don, the accountant, met her at the door of his office. "Congratulations on a great year," he began, "I've got good news and bad news for you. The good news is that you obviously had a sales increase. The bad news is that you owe taxes."

Pat sighed. "How much?"

He replied: "More than you have in your account, I'm afraid."

I was horrified. (Okay, this story actually happened to *me*.) In my giddiness over my increased sales, I hadn't paid enough attention to my inventory levels. It was my introduction to the importance of turn.

What is turn again?

As I said before, it refers to the number of times each year the inventory in your store sells out.

More turn is better, because every time you sell an item you recoup its costs plus earn the profit you need to pay yourself and your business expenses. Turn is determined over 13 months; it is more about the whole journey than it is about one three-month selling season.

The optimum turn varies for different stores and most importantly it varies for different types of inventory in a store.

For a toy store, it's about 3.5 times per year. For a quilt and fabric store, I want to see a turn of 2 times. The turn in a pet store is much faster because of the food side of the business.

No store should turn less than 2 times a year. The optimum turn means that you are maximizing your cash flow and getting more cash out of your store.

Let's say that your goal is to turn 3.5 times a year. That means merchandise should be sitting on your shelves for about 15 weeks (determined by dividing the number of weeks in a year – 52 – by the desired number of turns in a year – 3.5).

If an item is in your store for too long, it is turning too slow and not making the money it should for you. On the other hand, if you are constantly out of an item, it is turning too fast. You are missing opportunities for sales and thus losing money. Your goal is to find a balance and maximize the flow of cash for your store.

I had not maximized my cash flow. That is why I owed more money in taxes than I had in the bank. I immediately set out to increase my turn by decreasing my inventory.

Remember when I reminded you that turn is just a fraction and we talked about playing with the numbers to increase turn? That is just what I did.

Let's play with fractions! If 6/6 =1, and we wanted to increase the 1, we would keep less inventory – 6/2 = 3.

By decreasing my average inventory (which is the denominator of the fraction) I could increase my turn.

At that time, my sales were about $760,000 and my turn was only 2.7 times a year. So we take my sales of $760,000 divided by the 2.7 turn to get to $282,500 in average inventory at retail value.

To get to a turn of 3 times a year, we take the sales of $760,000 and divide by that 3 time turn so we see that I needed to get my inventory to about $253,300.

Now the trick is to reduce that inventory from $282,500 to $253,300. But I was motivated by getting my hands on some of that $29,200 that was sitting in inventory that wasn't moving out fast enough for me. I had to generate additional cash to pay that tax bill!

Digging Deeper

In June, I met with a client who was frustrated by his lack of cash flow. We identified one of the problems: His turn was too low.

By digging deeper, we discovered that the main culprit was a class of inventory called "building toys." As a rule, building toys *do* turn slower, more like 2.5 times, than the rest of the store. The rate of my client's building toy class was not even twice a year.

The turn of every store is determined by the sum of its classes. Each class or group of merchandise has a different turn. Each type of store has a different combination of classes, so they all have a different optimal turn rate.

Stores that carry teacher supplies *and* toys should consider the two separately. Toys turn at 3.5 and classroom supplies turn less frequently at about 2.5 or so.

Remember my theory – the stock-to-sales ratio is really about how much stock or variety of items customers need to evaluate before they make a decision to buy. Due to the quantity of choices necessary, customers of teacher stores require *more* merchandise to analyze before they purchase.

Take for example, a teacher that needs a math enrichment book. What grade? What type of math? What form of questions? There are so many variables that play into her decision. She needs to look at quite a few books before she buys one. You can see how that slows down the turn.

A turn rate of less than twice a year, like my client's building toys, indicates that merchandise that has been in the store for six months has to go *now*. My client and I ran a report to determine the specific slow-to-turn items and the results were fascinating.

First, we found several large building sets that had not sold during the previous holiday season. Hope springs eternal for the retail store owner, and my client was sure the items would sell *this* fourth quarter. I was concerned that they wouldn't, so we put a note on the calendar for the next December. If they haven't sold by then, we would mark them down immediately.

Our next discovery was a line of toys from the previous fall that hadn't sold well and was still in inventory. We marked them right down for my client's sidewalk sale in July.

The rest of the inventory was merchandise that would be ordered again eventually, but there was simply too much of it.

Soon we were able to focus on sales and discuss what could be done to increase business for the building toys category. My clients created a fantastic window display using products from a key vendor, and listed the benefits of playing with building toys on a sign in the background. They also scheduled two in-store play dates featuring building items.

Most importantly, I showed him that by speeding up his turn from 1.8 to 2.5 he would be able to put over $5000 into the bank. Without even increasing his sales!

$$\frac{66,000}{36,667} = 1.8 \qquad \frac{66,000}{26,400} = 2.5$$

He will maintain the same sales with $10,000 less inventory. How? Because he will have moved those slow selling inventory out and replaced it faster selling goods. At retail $10,000 is worth more than $5000 at cost. That's how much extra money he will have in the bank by paying attention to his turn.

Sales Down Boo! But Hooray Cash Was UP!

A client's sales had decreased $10,776. During the same time period, their turn had increased from 2.72 to 3.34.

It is easy to only see the decrease in sales here, I know. But let's look at the impact of the increased turn - which means that they were operating with less inventory.

That increase in turn meant that their average inventory decreased a total of $50,500 of inventory at retail. Based on their average initial markup (IMU) that translated into $23,735 more cash for them! That is why it actually PAYS to determine your turn.

Worth your effort

The most common complaint I hear is that turn seems too difficult to determine and is hard to grasp. Yes, it takes a little time and effort to figure it out, but I'm sure I was not the first, nor will I be the last store owner, to have that singularly stunning turn/tax experience. Many retailers don't understand clearly why or how turn impacts profit and cash flow. It controls the money that moves through your store and the money you get to keep in your pockets!

Turn, as a number, is meaningless if you look at it by itself. If you were to tell me much you weigh, I can't say if you are over or underweight unless I know other factors like your height, build, age and more.

In order to put more money in the bank, any store owner must know their turn rate in addition to gross profit, expenses, cost of goods percentage and more. Turn is a great tool for analyzing a store's success.

It's also a key consideration for tax planning, as I learned the hard way. Had I known my optimum inventory level, I could have prevented a high tax bill.

Take a look at your own turn. See what a difference it can make by increasing it just a bit. If you do $575,000 in business and your turn is 2, that means that your average inventory is $287,500. If you can increase your turn to 2.75, your average inventory decreases to $209,090.

That means that you can carry $78,410 less in inventory at retail value. At cost that is almost $40,000.

$$\frac{575,000}{287,500} = 2 \qquad \frac{575,000}{209,090} = 2.75$$

$$287,500 - 209,000 = 78,410$$

Wouldn't you like to have an extra $40,000?! You can do it utilizing the techniques that my client did.

Remember, merchandise is not like fine wine – it does not improve with age. It turns to vinegar... and stinks up the place!

Do not worry about losing a bit of profit now – we are concentrating on cash flow right this second. It is a fine line to walk. But most retailers err on the side of caring more about the profit and not moving the bad inventory out. Just like the story of the Christmas Urn!

Assignment:

1. Calculate your store's overall turn. Compare it to benchmarks for your industry.

CURRENT SALES

AVG INVENTORY AT RETAIL FOR 13 MONTHS = TURN

2. Determine your optimal inventory level to help your turn create the most profits for your store. YOUR goal using the formula:

CURRENT SALES

AVG INVENTORY AT RETAIL FOR 13 MONTHS = TURN

YOUR GOAL using the above formula:

Chapter Six
How to Ignore Your Customers:
Using Shock and Awe to Engage Your Raving Fans

"I once heard profit is the applause you get for taking care of customers and your people." Ken Blanchard

Ignore your customers.

You heard me right. Ignore them.

It is a fact that 80% of your sales come from 20% of your customers. I call them your raving fans.

Pay close attention to your raving fans. You can ignore the others much of the time. Not when they are in the store of course! But certainly in regards to your marketing and advertising.

Hold up your hands in front of you. Now bend your fingers down into your palm. What you have left is your raving fans – your thumbs. 2 out of every 10 customers are your raving fans.

Now open your fingers back up again and fold your thumbs in. Wiggle those 8 fingers. See how 8 out of 10 customers are NOT your raving fans.

It can get confusing because they tend to make more noise than your raving fans. They are the ones complaining about your pricing. They are the ones complaining about most everything. Handle them with respect and love but don't ever forget that they are NOT your raving fans.

Don't let one bad apple spoil the whole bunch.

Often, retailers make new policies because one of the "fingers" has taken advantage of something. Don't make a rule because of one jerk. Let it roll off you. Don't take it personally.

Return policies often happen because of what happened with one customer. Many policies – if not most – are put in place to protect the retailer or make procedures easier for the retailer.

What else is possible?

In my stores, we had a very liberal return policy. We would accept returns on full priced goods for 21 days for a full refund, and after 21 days we would give a store credit. We would accept sale priced goods back at any time for a store credit.

Why?

It was a kid's clothing store and we wanted to encourage moms to buy sale items for their kids to wear the next year. So we chose to remove the fear that they might be stuck with an item because they had incorrectly guessed their child's size for the next year. It was a policy developed with the customer in mind – and it absolutely increased sales.

I changed the policy once – to give customers cash back on gloves and mittens at any time with no questions asked.

Why?

One winter, I bought a spectacular coat with matching mittens for my 6-year-old daughter. It was a Nordic style coat in the most stunning rose color wool with amazing embroidery and had mittens to match. Caitlin looked adorable in it, but guess what happened in February? She lost one of the mittens.

I couldn't find any more mittens in any store! I live in Chicago. Winter lasts until May! This was a problem.

So the next year, my team and I told that story to customers that bought a coat and encouraged them to buy 2 pairs of mittens right then. I told them that we were instituting a "No Lost Mitten" Return Policy.

We would give cash back at any time if they didn't need the extra pair of mittens and decided to return them. They didn't even need their receipt.

What do you think happened? We sold dozens and dozens of additional mittens! And only had to refund 4 pair! It was a fabulous win-win situation for the customers and for us. We had provided a *solution* for their problem.

Many thanked us in the middle of winter because their child had lost a mitten and now they had an extra pair! Our "No Lost Mitten" return policy created good relationships and good retail.

Fire a Customer

Of course there are a few customers out there that buy and return and buy and return. Rather than develop a policy around them, you can choose not to sell to them. Really. You can.

The first thing to do is to stop marketing to them by removing their address information from your database. Leave their name in and insert a note about their behavior for your staff.

If that doesn't stop them from coming in, fire them.

I have done it. I once wrote a note to an abusive customer saying, "I have noticed that you have had many returns and our merchandise has not worked out for you and I am sorry about that. I know that it has cost you a great deal of time and effort, so it seems that we are not the right store for you. I am sure you would rather be shopping elsewhere and we wish you the best."

I never saw nor heard from them again.

As far as I know, there are no legal consequences to this action, but of course feel free to contact your attorney and ask. It worked like a charm for me.

How To Love On Your Thumbs – Aka Your Raving Fans

What else can you do to love on those wonderful people who generate about 80% of your sales? Invite them to be a part of your "club" for raving fans.

We love loyal customers. It is in rewarding those customers that we have the opportunity to turn them into raving fans. Don't miss that opportunity.

Loyalty programs are an essential way of acknowledging your appreciation for your customer's continued patronage and support with gifts and services of meaningful value. That chosen gift should not have any strings attached to it – otherwise it isn't freely given. It also should be able to be used immediately – which differentiates it from a bounce back coupon. (A bounce back coupon is a coupon given to a customer offering a discount on a purchase to be made within certain future time constraints.)

The goal is to reward your customers for making the right decision and choosing to shop with you. Look at your own behavior. Are you motivated only by discounts, miles or points? No. Those don't necessarily cause you to change your behavior and drive out of your way to go to a store.

Loyalty is inspired by the way that you make a difference in your customer's life in an important way. It will necessarily include a shock, surprise and awe component.

It isn't hard. You only need to know one thing. What matters to your best customers?

Go to your computer and pull up the list of your customers sorted by sales volume. Look at them. Picture them. What is important to them? What type of lifestyle do they lead? What do they buy from you?

Start a list. Force yourself to write down at least 25 entries. You will see commonalities. What could you gift them with that would make a meaningful impact?

For a toy store, it could be sending a great age appropriate gift to the customer's child on their birthday. The difference that makes is that you are recognizing the importance of their kids in their life – and you know that your customer will be impressed.

For a store that caters to brides you can give a special personalized gift when they do their registry with you. For a store with many moms on the go, your reward can be some sort of travel item that makes their life easier.

For any store, the reward could be tracking their purchases and giving them a percentage of that total back as a discount off of future purchase. This is certainly the most common way to reward them and is referred to as a frequent buyers/loyalty program.

Many of those programs give away more cash than they need to. Use an index card for each customer and write down each purchase (not including sales tax). After seven purchases, total up how much they spent and multiply it by 5%. That is then the value of the gift certificate that they have to use for their next purchase – which should be made within 30 days.

Take a new card and paperclip it to the old one so that you can easily determine who has an open gift certificate to use. On the front of the card, you have put the clients contact info. As it gets close to the end of the 30 days, you have the wonderful job of reminding them that they have a gift certificate to use at your store! You call and tell them that expiration date is approaching and ask them if they will be able to come in by then. If not, simply extend it for them. You look like a hero! And they love getting your gift of "free" money.

A side note to those who think this should be automated: Do not do it. Keep all these cards in a box. There is amazing social proof for other raving fans to see how many people shop with you.

Don't think that a successful loyalty program has to only be about giving inventory away. Never underestimate the value of specialized knowledge to someone who is pressed for time.

For a women's fashion store, your gift to a loyal customer could be a special report about the next season's must-haves – in all areas of fashion not just the ones that you sell. The report could include the latest trends in home accessories, colors and so on.

For a store that sells home décor or tabletop items, you can do the same thing.

If fashion and design is important to your best customers, then use your resources to pull together that information for them. They will be in awe of the fact that you are genuinely passing on knowledge that they care about – not just about items you have in your store.

Think outside of the box in delivering the loyalty gift. In a wine store, the owner could put together a report about a new vineyard or area of the world that is producing wines. Then she could record the report and make a podcast or send the customer a link to an mp3 recording. Think about what knowledge you have that you could share with your customer and how to share it.

Focus on the customer and their wants. That is the secret.

Your loyalty program must be selflessly focused on your best customers. That is what will shock, surprise and awe them. No one does that.

You will find that your customers are begging to award you their loyalty because it saves them time. They know where to go to get their need fulfilled – to your store. They already know, like and trust you. They want to shop with you.

If you reward them by making a difference and providing shock and awe, they will reward you with their continued loyalty and business.

Don't miss the opportunity to wish your raving fans a "Happy Birthday" with a no strings attached gift certificate to use the month of their birthday. Determine what your average sale for a year by taking your total sales volume and dividing it by the number of sales in the year. When you get that amount, multiply it by 20% and offer them that amount as a fun birthday gift. Again, you can always call to remind them.

Assignment:

1. Take a look at your return policy. Does it serve you or the customer? How can it serve both? I challenge you think about this further and revisit your return policy.

2. Is there a customer that you should fire? Name them.

3. This concept is so powerful. Invest the time and energy to discover what you can do. I suggest that you get two groups of people together: your staff and your top 10 customers. Both groups would have valuable insight on this topic.

· Do you send thank you notes?

· What do you see as the difference between excellent customer service and a fantastic customer experience?

· Be sure to ask for customer testimonials to provide social proof that your store is great!

- How can you "WOW" the customer the first time they walk through your door?

- Is there something you can do immediately following the sale to cement the great experience in their mind?

- What do you do well now? What could you do better? Analyze each cycle.

- What can you do or offer to show that you know they have choices and to thank them for shopping with you?

- Ask your customers what else you can offer to make their lives better – or to solve a problem in their lives – as it relates to what you do, of course!

- What could you offer to "encourage" them to tell their friends about you?

There are no wrong questions. The ONLY mistake is not doing anything.

Chapter Seven
Gather your Herd of Raving Fans
and Lead them in the Door

"Once the herd starts moving in one direction, it's very hard to turn it, even slightly." Dan Rather

If you aren't spending 20% of your time marketing, it doesn't matter how you are spending the remaining 80%.

You won't have a store.

Most retailers don't have a consistent method of interacting with their fans.

Most retailers don't have a marketing plan laid out. Without a marketing plan, you can end up not needing to order more inventory....or do all the other tasks that are keeping you from this all important job.

Every retailer must spend 20% of their time marketing, or it doesn't matter how they are spending the remaining 80%!

That's how you can get your marketing plan done!

Collect all information about every customer. Don't tell me that they don't like to share it. You are doing a bad job of asking for it. Your raving fans WANT to get information from you. You just have to ask for it in the right way.

Never ask if they want to be on your email list. You wouldn't want to give out your personal information be put on a list by a bored stiff employee. You would say no to that.

But what if you were invited to join a club with wonderful benefits at a store you like by someone who was enthusiastic?

That is the trick. No one wants to join a mailing list…but to be invited to be part of a club…that is a whole different story.

Let's break down how to do this. First, write out everything you do for those on your email list and a few extra benefits that you offer anyone!

- Free Giftwrapping
- Advance Notice of Fabulous Vendor Events
- First Chance at All Sales
- Double Loyalty Rewards Day
- Appointment Only Shopping Dates
- Private In-store Parties
- What else could *you* offer?

For a women's store, how about Professional Styling (as a gift to you) or a Closet Review. For a toy or gift or hobby store, All Special Orders at no charge. For a pet store, free nutritional analysis. For a quilt store, a discount on classes.

Put your list together and then frame it on your front counter so that you can point out to people all that you do as part of your club.

Next, call a team meeting to introduce this to your team. Tell them all about the fun club you're starting. Share all the benefits with them. Brainstorm other ideas of special events, experiences or services that you can offer. See if you can all come up with a name for it! Some call it a VIP club or YourName's Gang or XYZ Club.

Drive the Herd Through Your Front Door

You are forgettable. I hate to be the one to break it to you. This is the truth. People forget about you all the time. They are busy with their own lives and concerns. When they do think of you – it might not be about what you think it is.

We had been open for ten years and decided to do a little survey to our raving fans. What lines did they want us to carry? What lines did they not want to see anymore? What events they wanted to see?

We wanted to get some insight and direction from them. The very last question was "What is your favorite thing about Duck Duck Goose!?"

We gave them 4 options to choose from: our incredible selection, our fantastic team and customer service, the ability to buy toys, gifts, and clothing all in one place, and the 4th was a fill in the blank.

The three options we gave them were so obviously the right choice that we assumed they would choose all three. It was a shock to see the fill in the blank option was actually chosen the most. The overwhelming response was that their kids loved coming in and playing on our red climbing house.

That is not what we expected!! It certainly wasn't what was most important to us.

We realized what that meant to them. We had created an environment where they felt safe to let their precious kids play. They trusted us and it was a fun experience to come into the store. They didn't have to worry about their kids being yelled at for touching things. They could relax and shop. We were for the Child with Style who wanted to have fun too!

If you want to create more traffic through your front door, you have to be reminding them of who you are, what you want them to know and to share what is important to them.

How do you do this? How do you stay top of mind? You have to be emailing your raving fans every single week.

Every new client of mine complains about that and is worried that it is too much. But when they do it, they see that open rates rarely drop much at all. You don't realize how much your people love you! You will have a few more unsubscribes – but that is fine because you only want to talk to people who want to listen!

The reason open rates stay high is because my clients are loving on their raving fans in these emails. How? By giving them a gift. Every email is a G.I.F.T. - Genuine Information For Them.

You aren't always pushing a sale event. You know what your fans like and what is important to them – write about that in your emails. If you are a women's fashion store, tell them the latest trends, the hottest colors….and also what are the trendy haircuts and greatest shoes – even if you don't sell shoes! Talk about a toddler toy that Dad will play with too. Tell a story about repurposing gems at a jewelry store. Share a heartwarming Mother's Day story. The point is to give them information that they want and care about.

Make each email a G.I.F.T. Everyone wants to open a gift! That is why the open rates stay so high.

Think about that raving fan of yours, what do they care about so much that they might even lose sleep at night about it?

That is what you talk about and suggest items in your store that go along with those stories.

Who is the expert?

You are an Expert – You know more than you think you do. Think about why you started your store. You wanted to share your passion with others. I guarantee you that you have so much information about your passion.

You don't realize how valuable that information is to your raving fans. You know more than you realize and they want even the most basic of information. My client Sue and I were talking about classes to offer and I had her do classes for new quilters about putting colors together correctly. "Everyone know how to do that," she protested. "You are gifted at it." I told her. She thought that was too simple but indeed she sold the classes out!

Kim owned a dog store and grooming boutique and wanted more traffic. She was sure that she didn't know enough to do a class for her fans. "Why would they listen to me?" she said. Then we started talking about my dog, Riley, and an issue that Riley was having about food.

The first question Kim asked was about the condition of Riley's poop and then went on to share all you can learn about a dog's health from that! Who knew?

I convinced her to run a class for $10 per person in a local coffee shop and she got a great turnout. It served two purposes. It allowed her to state to her world that she was an expert and made her store stand apart from any other stores. The people who came learned so much and where do you think they are going to go when they have a question about their dogs? And she made $200 from it.

I spent time with Stephanie and her team coaching them on how they were true stylists. They all loved clothing and accessories and could put together outfits in their sleep practically. Through emails and social media, they kept talking about being stylists and how when you visited their women's clothing store they would help dress you up for work or for an important night out.

We did many before and after photos on mannequins that were shared with customers. This all served to build their credibility as a resource that improves their fans lives. They weren't just a women's clothing store. Their business grew 17% using this strategy.

We take for granted that information and skills that come easily to us must be the same for others. IT DOESN"T! Don't be selfish. Share your expertise with your raving fans.

Get Personal and Interesting

Make sure to include personal and fun information in your emails too. Your personal connection with your people creates more loyalty and more sales.

Stephanie was doing an email about New Year's Eve party styles and included her favorite Champagne drink recipe in it.

When Sue does emails for her gift store, she includes a "What's Hot" and "What's Not" section at the bottom. They usually reference her life or that of her team members. I remember one May she wrote: "What's Hot – My son graduating from U of I; What's Not – Long, boring commencement speeches"

Mike and his son would end every email from their toy store with a stupid and completely wonderful kid's joke! I always opened the email to read that joke. My favorite one is:

Q. Why did the monkey fall out of the tree?

A. It was dead.

That cracks me up every time!

All of these tactics create emails that people look forward to instead of dreading. You know how we usually can't open emails fast enough to delete them! Here they had people wondering "What is in this for me today?" That is what keeps them opening your emails….and opening your front door!

Trade Show Tips

You have an important opportunity here. You have ordered new things for your store. You walked all over those trade show floors looking for the latest and greatest trends. Then you analyze all your options and carefully edit your purchases. All this work is to perfectly translate those new styles into items that your customers will love and wear/use. Literally you have been working on this for months and it culminates very soon.

Notice I didn't say anything about selling them. Education is what is required here. The Encarta Dictionary defines education as "the imparting and acquiring of knowledge through teaching and learning."

Now it is time to educate your customers about those new trends you saw. Impart the knowledge that you now have about the season!

Share it with your customers. Use pictures. Use videos. Use a top ten list. Email your customers weekly. Update Facebook once a day with all this information.

You have so much to teach – so much to share with your customers. And they want to know! They count on you. Don't ever underestimate the value of being the expert and trusted source of knowledge for your customers.

Don't miss this – or your customers will go to your competition. Because your competition will follow through and put that information out if you don't. And I want your customers to hear about all the "new" from you first.

A big mistake would be to dismiss this tip by thinking it is only for clothing and shoe stores. It is true that they have a HUGE opportunity. For sure, every woman wants to be 'on trend'! We are at the front edge of this fashion and not every woman knows that yet. You have the unique position of knowing what that trend is. So it is your job to educate them and get them to buy it from you first.

However, every gift and toy store can find the same type of "trend" within your special niche. What is the newest gift item that will make your customers look like a gift giving rock star? For toy stores, there are a number of new games that your customers don't know about yet- and those big box stores don't have anyone who can tell you anything about them There is something new in every category of merchandise.

Assignment:

Identify 6 trends and/or items in your store that you didn't know about in the beginning of the year. Find 6 new things that your customers need to know about. Then start educating. Your customers will thank you!

Oh, and the top 3 things you must do to have a profitable season...

1. Educate your customer.

2. Educate your customer.

3. Educate your customer.

And then repeat!

Chapter Eight
A Love Letter to You From Your Raving Fans

Good Morning, My Favorite Retailer!

I want you to take a moment and think about the lives that you impact every single day through the work that you do.

I want you to take a moment and think about the memories that have been created because of the items that families have used from your store.

I want you to take a moment and think about the big happy smiles that birthday boys and girls, birthday moms and dads, birthday men and women have grinned because of the gifts that someone that loved them got from your store.

I want you to take a moment and think about the huge hugs that have been shared because of gifts purchased at your store. I want you to think of the hearts overflowing with gratitude and happiness because of an item that you carefully selected and someone else shared!

I want you to take a moment and think about the beautiful looks and kind thoughts that a 'getter' of an item from your store has bestowed on the 'giver' of the item from your store.

I want you to take a moment and think about the "Please forgive me – I am a jerk" gift from your store that softened someone's heart.

I want you to take a moment and think about the good news that was shared through an item in your store – like the gift of a Mickey Mouse stuffed animal surprising a family with a trip to Disneyworld.

I want you to take a moment and think about the confidence you gave someone when they wore that fabulous outfit that you helped style for them.

I want you to take a moment and think about the opportunity that you gave somebody to share their love with another through a purchase of a perfect gift from your store.

Think about the lives impacted, memories created, smiles smiled, hugs shared, looks bestowed, hearts softened, news shared, confidence given, love flowed … All because you opened your store.

Thank you! I know some days are hard and I am here to remind you today of why you do what you do.

It makes a difference in the life of another person.

Thank you. Sending you grace and joy today!

Happy Retailing….really!

Chapter Nine
Dump Your Big Dreams:
You Must Think Bigger to Be Bigger

*"Act the way you'd like to be and
soon you'll be the way you'd like to act."* Bob Dylan

You're reading this book to make a change, and what I want you to realize is that there are so many things that you're doing right already. There really are. I always talk about how there's art and a science in retail. I've got the science down cold and that's what I'm bringing to you. The art is what to buy, and that is what you're good at.

We're not going to talk about that. What I'm going to be talking about is the science of retail, so that you can get more profits.

I also want to be able to talk about you having more fun and getting better sleep and that's the reason why I really want to go through that exercise of thinking through what is it, what are the personal lifestyle goals you have.

And what are the money goals you want for this store? And what is it you'd like to be able to create for yourself this next year? That's what I'd like you to be able to do.

The biggest mistake retailers make is having big dreams. They think that one day they will have a nationwide chain of stores. They dream about someone buying them out and hiring them to just carry out their message across the country in stores all over.

You have to dump those big dreams.

The secret is to THINK bigger. Think about a goal that is just out of your reach. Think of a $500,000 store. Think of a $1,000,000 store. Think of a $5,000,000 store. Try one of those thoughts on for size. Which one is exciting and truly achievable for you in the next few years? Now CLAIM IT. You ARE that size store now.

Breathe that in. You are a $1,000,000 store. Visualize it.

What would you do differently than you do right now?

More importantly, what would you NOT do? What would you be delegating? That is what trips most people up.

Your store can't grow any bigger than you allow it to. If you are holding onto every detail because you do it best, then you will always be limited by the amount of time in your day. Even if you committed 18 hours a day for 6 days a year, you would only have 5616 hours to get things done in the store. That isn't enough time to get to that next level you want to get to.

When you delegate, you are multiplying your time. If you bring in 1 person for 20 hours a week for the year that is an additional 1040 hours spent getting things done. As more gets done, your sales and profits grow.

Let go and grow.

No matter if you claimed the $500,000 or $5,000,000 think bigger store idea, you can learn from this exercise. Write down every task that you do in the store today. What of those things can ONLY be done by you? Not which of those things are best done by you. Not which of those things did you have to do because no one did them. Not which of those things did you do because no one else even notices. All of that is simply a problem with your training and expectation process.

When I have clients look at it this way they always find tasks that others can do for them. Then that opens them up to work on the really important core growth strategies for the store. That is where their time and energy is best spent. Because that is what grows stores and lives.

Think about the kind of things you would want to do differently IN your store if you were that store?

What would you do differently for your raving fans?

How would your marketing and advertising calendar look?

At every level of your "think bigger store idea," you will grow more by answering these questions. Actually, that isn't true. You won't grow by answering the questions. You will ONLY grow by acting on and IMPLEMENTING the answers.

What? You have no time to do that? We are right back where we started. Make the time.

I remember Meme and Bree first struggled with this when we started working together. They had no employees, no sales growth no cash and were burnt out. "How can we afford to hire anyone?" That was their question.

We started with 10 hours a week. Meme and Bree had to promise me that they would both use those 10 hours per week to work on sales generating activities. That time couldn't be used to do any tasks. They could only do activities that would generate sales immediately.

Bree started to work on their weekly email. They had never had time to follow through with that before. Meme spearheaded an effort with one of their best vendors to do a trunk show event.

Together they spent time brainstorming ideas to make the event better than ever. One idea that came out of it was inviting their best customers for that vendor to an early morning "Mimosa Preview Party" of the line. They also decided to raffle off a "in store private party" with the line to one of those customers. That was brilliant.

The customer could have a fun girls' night out in the store after hours with food and drink plus have her best friends come and shop in Meme and Bree's store. Talk about a win-win situation! That successful event would never have happened if they hadn't committed the time to sales generating activities.

They were able to easily meet payroll for that 10 hours of time. It happened because they spent that time working on sales generating activities that they never would have been able to otherwise. The true beauty of this is that it just builds.

My Million-Dollar Retail Store

Think about what your million-dollar retail store looks like? If money was no object, what are the kind of things you'd like to do? Think big. I want you to think of what you would do, and what you would not do, if money was no object. Let your mind go wild and think about all this. I want to see what ideas you come up with.

So many wonderful ideas come from this.

I had one retailer add a whole other income stream to her business. One of the great ways to generate money is to look for additional income streams. This woman was talking about how she really loves doing tabletop designs – she calls them "tablescapes." And it comes so easy to her. The things that come easiest to you, the things that are your unique ability, those are the things that it is really your duty to share with other people.

She has a gift store, so I talked to her about creating classes and teaching other people what comes so easily to her. She said, "No one is going to want to know how to do that!" I replied, "Yes, they are! They absolutely are going to want to know!"

It's not something that comes naturally to people. It's been such a cool thing to see and it's a wonderful addition to her income stream for her company.

That additional revenue doesn't only come through selling things. Maybe there's something that you'd just love to do in your store. I had a kid's store that decided to add doing birthday parties, and then they decided to add doing play groups, and now they're doing diapering sessions. And making money from each new activity.

I have another store that also has book clubs in their store, not just where the reader reads, but they actually have book clubs in their store. That's just an adorable idea, just a wonderful, different way of using your store.

The idea of a book club came out of the fact that the owner really loved to read. She loved book clubs and she really liked some of her customers and that's what she wanted to do.

So that's what I want you to do – not only dream big and think big about it, but turn those dreams into action.

Assignment:

1. List what can only you do:

2. Take another look at that list – delegate half of it:

3. Where else can you utilize other's special skill sets?

4. What do you not want to ever have to do again?

5. Who are you going to give those tasks to?

6. What revenue generating activities will you do first?

Chapter Ten
Don't Join the Retail Fire Brigade:
Take Control of Your Time and Accomplish Your Goals

The key is in not spending time, but in investing it.
Stephen R. Covey

There are two reasons you can't get anything done and aren't getting the results that you want.

The Retail Time Warp

Being in retail is like being in an emergency room. There is an emergency or a fire to be put out at any moment.

It is an "interruption rich" environment.

As in every pert of retail, there is a science to this that you have to learn to be able to take control of this "Retail Time Warp Zone." I have certainly been there and experienced it. That feeling when you look at the clock and realize that the store closes in 15 minutes and you got nothing done. AND you are exhausted. There is a pile of paperwork you have to bring home again. All that mail that still needs to be opened and those reorders to be taken care of.

You walk through the back door and realize that you need to order more shipping tape when you see the three open boxes still sitting there from yesterday. Then there is a list of customer requests taped to the back of your chair. You make a pit stop in the bathroom first and see that there is no more hand soap. As you walk out on the floor, you see that you are almost out of a favorite item of yours, so you grab it to remind yourself to reorder it. On the counter you pick up a note telling you to return a call from a sales rep. You walk back to your desk with your hands and mind full of things to do.

You are so distracted you don't know where to start.

It's okay. You suffer from Retail ADD. It's a clinical problem. Let's blow it up.

Use TNT to blow up retail ADD

You have to prioritize and focus to get the results that you want. I can teach you to use TNT to get explosive results!

T – Top Three Identify the three most important and impactful actions you can take to generate more sales today. Just three to start with. Write them down. Then take the critical step of scheduling exactly when you will do them.

N – No Email Do not open up your email until you have accomplished the above three tasks have been completed or scheduled out. Your inbox is often just someone else's list of things for you to do. Take control and don't let that happen.

T – Timer Use a time to hyper-focus and knock those items off your list. Set it for a time period that is between 15 and 45 minutes. Then get to work. Don't look at the timer again. Take any distracting thought captive and throw it out. When the timer goes off, stop. Take a break. Then repeat.

This simple strategy gives you the control back over your time. It makes it easier to focus on what has to get done to increase sales. Those important items are often not the most urgent. And the most urgent items can be put off for a bit so that you can focus on the most important items that will move your store closer to your goal.

Don't Let Excuses Keep You From Getting What You Want

Excuses are another culprit in keeping you from getting done what you want to. Either excuses that you tell yourself or ones that you believe about your customers. Those excuses are the reason that their customers didn't come through the door. You have to create urgency and focus for your customers to EVER walk through your door.

I have heard retailers say that they couldn't reach a sales goal because of the weather. That is absolutely crazy. Oh I can hear you moaning and groaning now.

"Cathy, you just don't understand the winter we had."

"You haven't seen rain until you saw what happened last weekend. No one came in."

We are always looking for reasons for things, right? But working with so many retailers at the same time, I can tell you that I have stores on the same street that can have completely different sales results with exactly the same weather.

One of my most successful semi-annual clearance sales was on the day of a massive snowstorm. I remember driving to the store with my kids (because school had been cancelled) and swearing the whole way there because I was sure no one would show up. Imagine my shock when we had an amazing day. Customers said that it was the end of Christmas break, their husband's offices were closed and they had to get out of the house! The urgency was that the sale was that day and the focus was that they wanted out!

Retailers will tell me that they can't sell winter coats in July. That's an excuse. We did an annual winter coat trunk show in the first week of July that was very successful. Kids would come in from swim class with their suits on and hair wet to try on coats. The urgency was that it was an incredible selection only offered at that time and the focus was that they would need a winter coat that year for sure.

I teach my clients to look at a sales goal for a whole month. So even if one day is bad, you still have time to DO something to get more business in the other days.

Do not fall prey to the idea that your raving fans won't shop with you because they are too busy. Make sure that you are giving them a reason to shop with you. *Urgency* and *focus* must be created to get people through the front door.

I had a women's store client who always said people wouldn't shop during August – and she was right. Her sales stunk every August. I would tell her that every women's store was doing good business but she refused to change her mindset about it. One year she was in a bit of a cash crunch and NEEDED to have a good August. We created a "Fall Preview Day" event that made her fans crazy about spending their dollars with her. We held quite a few of the fall shipments back and put them out one day for all to shop. They were left in the plastic wrap and put on rolling racks. Sweaters were left in boxes for the fans to look through. Everything was tagged to be sure. It ended up generating 64% of the entire month's business on the ONE DAY! And now it is a tradition and people wait for it. Now she also allows her top customers to come in the day before….they feel so special and taken care of and they buy!

The most important lesson is that she no longer allows excuses to keep her from getting the sales she wants

What are you doing to create Urgency and Focus?

Assignment:

1. Use TNT to blow up your retail ADD – today!

T=

N=

T=

2. Create urgency and focus in your store – no excuses!

Chapter Eleven
Getting Information and Not Taking Action
Will Cost You Your Business

*"We are what we continually do. Excellence, therefore, is not
an act but a habit."* Aristotle

Why what you *do* matters.

Did you intend to run a not for profit business? If not, you need
to support yourself and those who love you.

Getting info and not taking action is stupid. You must take
action in order to see the results you want. Just knowing what you
should do, having the right ideas, and being brilliant and wonderful
are note enough. Let me tell you about Julia.

Phone calls

This is an actual conversation that I had with a retailer ...

"Cathy, my business stinks. What can I do?"

"I would love to help you. Send me some information so that I
can see what strategy you should take to explode your profits. In
the meantime, can I give you ***one REVENUE-BUILDING-
GUARANTEED tip***?"

**"Please anything...I will do anything...the store is full of
fantastic items but devoid of customers and I have so many
bills!"**

"OK. Run a list of your top 100 customers from your point of
sale system to see when they were in last and what they bought.
Take each one individually, and compare their last purchases to
what you have in the store now. I am sure that you have items that

would complement or supplement what they bought before. Then call them to tell them about these great items that you chose especially just for them!"

"Oh no...I wouldn't want to bother them and I don't have time to do that. It would take forever to do that."

"You just said you have no customers – so you have time to fill. **You said you want more sales, right?** My other suggestion is to email them with a personal note and you could send a photo."

"Oh but I don't have their email addresses."

"Well, then call them and tell them that you want to send them a photo of the most fabulous thing that you really think that they will love and all you need is their email!"

"Oh no, I can't call them."

"Think about this. If you could tell a specific customer that you have a specific item that you have specifically chosen for them because you honestly think that they will like it. If you called to say, "Hi Ashley, this is Cathy from The Best Shop. Hey, I don't want to bother you at all and just had one quick thing to tell you – is that ok? (***Big Huge Note Right Here – You asked for permission to continue!***) Well, I was noticing that when you were in last you bought this thing and I just found this other thing that would be fabulous with it and would make you be able to use the first thing twice as much!...... If you called to tell them just that – I mean **what are you afraid of?**"

"That I will make them mad and they will yell at me and call me names and scream at me that they don't need what I am selling."

"Really? Would you act like that if someone called about something specific like I outlined above?"

"Well, I might not want what they think I might want."

"That is true – and that is fine! But would you really be mad? And scream? And curse?"

My dear reader, this is where the serious retailers are separated out from the hobbyist retailers. It becomes clear who is willing to do WHATEVER it takes to achieve their goals versus who is only going to do WHAT IS CONVENIENT. This is the point that divides those who just want to complain and those who just want to put money into the bank.

Which are you?

Assignment:

1. Run a list of your top 100 customers from your point of sale system to see when they were in last and what they bought. Take each one individually, and compare their last purchases to what you have in the store now. I am sure that you have items that would complement or supplement what they bought before.

2. Then call them to tell them about these great items that you chose especially just for them!

Chapter Twelve
Don't Go It Alone:
Put an Expert In Your Corner

"I am not a teacher, but an awakener." Robert Frost

I HATE FAILURE.
I LOVE SUCCESS. How about you?

It is essential for every person who is serious about achieving significant personal and business growth to work with a coach. That is a fact. You can't do it on your own. Every successful athlete depends on a coach because they know it is the only way to successfully grow and improve their performance. Your performance in your store is no different.

I have a coach. We recently developed an action plan that included the execution of this one particular activity. Everything else stemmed from that. I agreed to it. It didn't look scary. It didn't seem so big. But I had a heck of a time executing it. I couldn't figure out why.

It was so hard that I really fell into a deep hole of anxiety about it – which made accomplishing other work very difficult. I sat in that hole and couldn't figure out what the heck the problem was. It just didn't seem so difficult – but I was totally stuck. I couldn't move.

Why?

I was afraid I would fail. I came to realize that my hatred of failure stopped me dead in my tracks.

My big a-ha moment was recognizing that I was actually deathly afraid of failure.

 As my coach guided me through this I saw clearly that it is because I am afraid to look "less than". Do you know what I mean? I will look less than perfect…less than successful. It is much more fun to look successful! Even if it is a lie.

When God wants you to get a message, He will send it to you multiple times. Often, I get hit on the head with it! That is certainly what happened to me.

First, my coach and mentor kept challenging me. I kept telling her that she was wrong. Fear of failure isn't my problem I insisted.

Next, I read "Managing Yourself: The Paradox of Excellence" by Thomas DeLong and Sara DeLong published in the Harvard Business Review.

"High achievers often let anxieties about their performance compromise their progress. Because they're used to having things come easily to them, they tend to shy away from assignments that test them.…They have successful images to preserve, so instead of embracing risk, they hunker down …at the expense of personal growth."

At first I dismissed this point. I like to learn new things. I don't care what people think of me.

But then why was I so anxious? This had to be true. And it is. I know that I don't like to fail and so I don't test myself. *"First, you have to take a hard look at yourself and identify the forces that escalate you anxieties and cause you to turn to unproductive behaviors for relief…you must adopt practices that give you courage to step out of your comfort zone, "* the DeLongs report.

Unproductive behaviors that give me relief.....does that mean Facebook? Playing games on my phone? Watching TV too long into the night? The truth was right there. I couldn't ignore it.

My accountability partner challenged me about not following through. (Accountability partner? Yes, it is imperative to have support around you when you have big dreams.) "What are you afraid of? Are you afraid you aren't good enough to do this? Really? After all the success your clients have had over the decade of consulting with you?"

"Yes," I said.

We all have a crisis of confidence from time to time. We all have our highs and lows, our ups and downs. We weather them and keep going. They pass.

The DeLongs state *"It's hard to exorcise past demons until you have looked at them dispassionately from multiple points of view. Almost without exception, overwhelming feelings of inadequacy are in our own minds."*

Our fears are only in our minds.

The final message from God came via Derrick Rose. While watching the Chicago Bulls play a couple of years ago, I saw the statistic that 31 of their 103 points came from second chance shots. Nearly a third of their points came because the first shot failed and they tried again.

I can do that. I can embrace failure and try again and then succeed.

I had failed to reach my sales goal. I was mad. I realized that I could have blamed my coach. There were many factors I could have pointed to. But really the problem was that I hadn't followed through on our action plan. I had stalled. If I hadn't worked through this issue I would have stayed stuck. She hadn't failed....I had to exorcise my demons.

*"To achieve continued success, you must open yourself up to new learning experiences that many make **you feel uncertain at <u>best</u> and incompetent at <u>worst</u>**. Remember that those feelings are temporary and a prelude to greater ability,"* the DeLongs encourage.

I took action and I broke my new venture down into steps and have met with much greater success than I thought! I blew my sales goal out of the water!! YAY!! It all comes from my passionate desire to help retailers like yourself get more profit and love your life. Just wait until you see all I have planned!

Here's the thing, I got through all of this with help. If I didn't have that help, it is likely that I would never have gotten to this point. If your first shot didn't make it through the hoop and you are ready for a second shot with some help, contact me at <u>cathy@retailmavens.com</u>. Let's do a VIP day together.

Assignment:

1. What are you afraid of? Write it down, take away its power.

2. Find an accountability partner – how can you help each other be accountable to your goals?

3. Find a coach! Your first shot may have missed, but a coach can help you win the game with your second!

Afterword

It's oh so hard.

It is. I am reminded daily that if this were easy everyone would do it.

The phone calls.
The late night emails.
The customers who want everything just right and make you crazy.
The customers who can't make decisions so they really need you.
The hiring of good help.
The hours.
The risk.

So, why do you do it? You are super smart, willing, and hard working. You could be employed and keep things simple.

Why?

The movement. It can be your tagline and you can still sometimes forget.

We have something to say.
We need a lot of space to say it.
We are creative.

We want to share the beauty we see with others.
We are a little nuts.
We are dreamers.

We are the ones that keep the employees dreams alive.
We are the ones who care so much we take the hard road.

WE have something to change.

So, for those of you pulling a late night or an early morning... for those finishing an order... or texting a sales rep… tagging the latest shipment... or writing your next marketing email... for those of you delivering more than you promised... for those of you digging deep to give back more... for those of you risking it all... for those of you innovating... for those of you doing it despite the fear...

THANK YOU. We all need you.

www.ingramcontent.com/pod-product-compliance
Lightning Source LLC
Chambersburg PA
CBHW071454200326
41519CB00019B/5726